The Squannacook at Dawn

Richard Jordan

First Place Winner of The Poetry Box Chapbook Prize 2023

Poems © 2024 Richard Jordon
All rights reserved.

Editing & Book Design by Shawn Aveningo Sanders
Cover Image licensed via RawPixel
Cover Design by Shawn Aveningo Sanders
Author Photo (p.35) by Sarah Jordon

No part of this book may be republished without permission from the author, except in the case of brief quotations embodied in critical essays, epigraphs, reviews and articles, or publisher/author's marketing collateral.

First Place Winner of The Poetry Box Chapbook Prize 2023
ISBN: 978-1-956285-49-9
Published in the United States of America.
Wholesale Distribution by Ingram Group

Published by The Poetry Box, February 2024
Portland, Oregon, United Sates
website: ThePoetryBox.com

The Squannacook at Dawn

Contents

Casting from Shore	7
First Caddis	8
Jesus on the River	9
The Art of Topwater Fishing	10
Mackerel Day	11
With the Current	12
[I lift the trout fly]	13
Home from the River	14
Night Fishing with Otters	15
Upon Reading the Local Pages	16
Old Men Fishing, with Osprey	18
Happy Meals	19
Spillage	20
Returning to Vermont	21
Exit 37B	22
Blackbird through October Mist	23
Ice-Out	24
What Was There	25
The Squannacook at Dawn	26
Casting from Shore (II)	27
Acknowledgments	29
Early Praise	31
About the Author	33
About The Poetry Box Chapbook Prize	35

Casting from Shore

A red-winged blackbird and the empty bottle
of Bud my father tilts to catch the breeze
bring music to the air this final day
of summer, and while trophies have been scarce—
no bass biting, only small white perch—
I know they're out there somewhere, possibly
beyond the island where lily pads
grow thick, where mergansers dive, where other
kids with other fathers have drifted in
new fiberglass canoes, the kind we can't
afford. But, nonetheless, we're here today
while they are not. And soon, real soon, I'll reach
that spot. I'll craft the perfect cast. *Hold on*,
my father says. He bends to trace a cross
on my tanned forehead with his free hand, then
points skyward as I launch the bobber high,
aimed to split a cloud, the way he taught.

First Caddis

Musty fur and rusted hook, this is
my oldest elk hair caddis, the first fly
my father let me tie myself. He lifted it
to the lamp, said, *This will do.* And yes,

it raised a bright, native speckled trout
from Trapfall Run, like I'd only seen
before in *Field & Stream*. My father took
the fish from my line, placed it in my hands,

but it shook free, slid down the gravel bank
back into the water. I watched it dart away,
splashing across a riffle to a shaded pool
beyond my casting reach. *Don't worry,*

where there's one... he said, striking
a match against an oak to light his pipe,
an iridescent scale glued to his thumb
glinting in the April morning sun.

Jesus on the River

Sometimes he thinks he should enter the church, but the river holds him, with kingfishers that rattle back and forth across a quiet pool, slate-blue wingtips almost dipping in, more graceful than clergy. From a boulder in the middle of the pool, he can see parishioners go through the doors. They are small from up there, like dolls. Meanwhile, he admires the way a trout faces the current to breathe and consume what's delivered by the flow—that would make a good sermon, he imagines. It's the one he would give.

The Art of Topwater Fishing

Do you ever make the ideal cast,
thread the gap between two lily pads,

then let the popper undulate and settle,
maybe fiddle with your visor, take

a look skyward? Maybe geese float over
without honking. Maybe while you look,

you listen to the snap of bluegills snatching
dragonflies that flutter close. Perhaps

it's warm, but no one's mowing, and the buzz
is the work week's murmur fading from your ears,

by then soft enough that you make out
an osprey calling high above the maples.

Say a scent like tangerine from sweet flag
is drifting past you, and you may detect

the glandular message a muskrat left behind
for other muskrats. When you finally give

your line a twitch from habit, does the plop-
chug of the lure startle you a little?

Perfect. Take a breath and let the surface
find its glassy state again. Repeat.

Mackerel Day

It's a mackerel day, my father used to say, when the lighthouse far off on the island disappeared and fog swirled thick and low over the breakwater, my father puffing his cognac pipe tobacco, me wearing his old red baseball cap, the two of us standing on slick rocks threading silver treble hooks with clams, seagulls circling closer and closer, they knew we'd save some bait, with the moan of a ship out there somewhere or maybe a whale, and I'd ask when the lighthouse would come back and flash, *soon*, and my father was always right, and sometimes—often—I still wake at dawn with a taste of salt air tingling my tongue.

With the Current

We're at the Squannacook again. The trout
are stirring as my father leans against
a willow, watches dimpled rings emerge

where open mouths poke through the surface, pluck
drowning damselflies. We've come to choose,
perhaps simply imagine the perfect spot

to spread his ashes when he's gone. *This place
right here*, he says. Yes, this place where he taught
me to cast upstream and let the river

present the fly the natural, dead-drift way.
Stay with the flow. The current feeds the trout
what arrives. A rainbow leaps. Another.

My father takes a step toward the water,
bends to dip a finger, slowly rises.
We're not here to fish today. We left

the car in idle, steady hum reminding
us to go and do what might need doing
this bright May morning, now approaching noon.

[I lift the trout fly]

I lift the trout fly
as my father did
to early morning light—
a perfect cinnamon sedge
the last he ever tied

Home from the River

dad's ashes
smudged on mom's cheeks

she'd never know

the old retriever
greeted her
washed them away

Night Fishing with Otters

Is it curiosity, or an urge
beyond me that attracts them to the gurgle
of my surface lure, that battered, vintage
Jitterbug? On clear, dark evenings, eyes

glow and flicker in the beam of light
from the lamp strapped to my forehead—five
otters at the edge of sedge and bulrush
measuring my slightest twitch. Often,

the young swim out to open water, circle,
plunge, resurface, each time closer to
the dock from which I cast for largemouth bass.
Occasionally, they'll chatter a few feet

away from me. Their mother answers with
a chuckle from the reeds. But, only once
has she emerged. She dove and quickly popped
back up, a hefty, flapping catfish plucked

from mud, clenched firmly in her jaws, as if
to show those who watched the way it's done,
then paddled off beyond the lily pads,
old Jitterbug wobbling slowly in her wake.

Upon Reading the Local Pages

Hi again, Mrs. Gladys Peters, born
in Groton, Massachusetts in 1940,

known to friends as Glad, although I won't
call you that, since we met only once,

when I was young. It was April 1980,
I think. A warm Saturday, I'm sure

of that. A cloud of mayflies hovered over
a clear pool. A scent—a spice like clove—

wafted from a shrub with lipstick-pink
blossoms. I'd just hooked a large, tenacious

stump and was about to cut my line
when you appeared beside me in a cobalt

sweater and straw hat. You asked, *What's biting?*
Nothing yet, I said. You breathed in deep,

smiled and declared, *They're something else,*
these azaleas. Then wandered down the path.

But Mrs. Gladys Peters, née Ahearn,
wife to Corporal Franklin Peters (deceased,

1969), survived by Cousin John
in Selkirk, Manitoba, I must tell you

I stayed until late afternoon. And there
were native brookies, olive-green and speckled

gold. So, thank you, Mrs. Gladys Peters.
I now understand it was your stone

wall I stumbled over to find trout.
I landed one. A small yet shining beauty.

Old Men Fishing, with Osprey

There are mornings nothing breaks the surface,
no bass or pickerel tug their fishing lines.
So, they talk to pass the time, perhaps
about the touchdowns they scored way back when,

wars they fought in, or wars their grandkids now
fight, obituaries. But sometimes
an osprey circles overhead and they fix
their sights on feathers fanned out wide, watch

it ride the wind, slice right through stubborn clouds.
They forget what they were saying, even why,
It's all about the majestic dive to come,
always claws-first, shattering the quiet,

the osprey rising with a glistening trophy,
the likes of which they've longed for their whole lives.

Happy Meals

Grandpa once gutted the scrawny perch I netted,
grilled the slivers in cornmeal and butter, salted
and buried them between thick layers of lettuce
served on bulky rolls to fool my stomach.

Today I slice his Filet-O-Fish into cubes
and set aside for him my smallest fries.
I ramble on about Otter Lake that summer.
He studies his knuckles' knotted veins and says,

New Hampshire. Something sparks this time, at least,
and I'm grateful that an otherwise forgettable
dab of tartar sauce on his Sunday tie
still makes him good and mad, like I remember.

Spillage

Searing August evening and the river has congealed
to a wary crawl. There are no herons stalking shiners,
not a single kingfisher in sight. There's only
Ramsdell snoring, Old Grand-Dad oozing

from his pores, taped cane pole propped
up by a wishbone twig. The lone sucker
in his rusted bucket hasn't gasped for hours.
And Ramsdell—does he conjure in a drunken dream

a fevered boil of shad, the flashes of sleek rainbow trout
not seen since the dam downstream yawned and choked
two years ago? Even now a stand of stunted oaks
stays sunken along the bank. A dozen limbs break

through the waterline, like the arms of pilgrims
at the point where it's not yet clear who's cleansed
or who's drowning, or how long it takes
a soiled river to cure. Yet—Ramsdell inhales deep,

then belches. And perhaps it's just a spastic twitch,
but the insinuation of a smile sharpens the creases
of his eyes when a bullfrog upstream issues its reply,
hoisting a brassy *jug-o-rum* to the haze.

Returning to Vermont

Could've sworn I'd find the place by heart,
the deep, clear pool we once chanced upon
where, splashing loud and naked, we flushed out

a rainbow trout long as a forearm from
its shade between the bank and polished stones.
This will always be our spot, she said. It was

early October then, as now, but what's
become of the sunlit pumpkin field, the ripe
Macouns that spiced the air? Already north

of Stowe, I should've passed the cedar fence,
the Holsteins stretching their long tongues to taste
the other side. I'm lost, though I won't turn

around. How to explain? Ahead, the leaves
and sky fuse burgundy with fuchsia. See,
she used to paint. She could have painted that.

Exit 37B

The house stood near a widening of the creek.
It was gray, small, maybe fifty feet back
from the bulrush bed where pearl dace glittered
when the sun climbed high. A freeway overpass

now casts its shadow across that place. The bank
is choked with loosestrife. But I knew a woman
who lived there twenty years ago. I trimmed
her forsythia, planted peas & later worked

my line along a riffle on a day
when brook trout broke the surface at the suggestion
of a damselfly. We breaded the pink fillets:
cornmeal, salt, a drizzle or two of ale

& they tasted delicious, out there in the open.
Like spring, we thought, like nothing you could buy.

Blackbird through October Mist

Water warmer than the air, the mist
swirling as you dip the paddle in
to navigate the narrow bend, and then

comes the throaty *check-check-oak-a-lee*
rising from the cattails. You imagine
red and golden epaulets aflame,

like the leaves whirlpooling in your wake,
but only see a shadow flitter through
the reeds. His song will soon be gone for months,

lost to snow and ice. It is important
now to lift the paddle, let it rest
across your lap. This is the time to glide.

Ice-Out

This morning two young boys came riding by
my house on bicycles, waving fishing poles,
splashing through fresh puddles from March melt.

I could hear them way down the road: such laughter,
a shout or two, more laughter. Red-winged blackbirds
went silent as the boys sped past, but shortly

started back strong with their *check check check*,
then a chipmunk shimmied up the feeder post,
the first I've seen since well before Thanksgiving.

At the lake, the channel ice has broken. It flows
away through the culvert. Fish hang deep, likely
won't chase a lure in such frigid water. Still,

the boys came riding, causing a fleeting commotion.
They'll surely grow someday to understand patience
and these ancient patterns. I pray it's no time soon.

What Was There

Netted three sleek native brookies, spots
and pelvic fins the brightest red I've ever seen.
Released them back into the clear swift water.
Hiked a mile to get to that place, over

the last remnants of snow, a little ice.
Bushwhacked the final half through bramble
and twisted vines. Waded another mile, at least,
across slick stones. Once there, just me all day,

along with two young mallards, a kingfisher,
a dozen or so fluttering spring azures,
momentarily a mink, a small gurgling
waterfall. Smelled sweet smoke drifting by,

like the purest maple sap boiling down—yes,
there must be a sugar house in heaven.

The Squannacook at Dawn

Where the riffle spills across smooth cobble
then slows to fill this quiet pool, the moon,
undulating on the surface, slips
through my fishing net. Another rainbow
trout has shaken loose, But, oh, that cool
splash of water on my face, that great
horned owl asking who. As usual,
it's me twitching my old caddis fly
to find whatever's stirring at first light,
not bothered that my creel is empty. See,
no matter where I go from here today
the river will be with me. Let it flow.

Casting from Shore (II)

I loved the arc, the droplet spray, the swish.
The orange floater cut through clouds then splashed
where dark water held the trophy cats—
hornpout, bullhead. Prehistoric fish,

it seemed to teenage me. I'd load my hook
with aged chicken liver, skipping Mass
on warm Sunday summer mornings, cast,
wait for the plunge and dream a little, look

around. It was a ritual passed on
by my dad. Sometimes I'd see a stray
canoe out past the island slip away,
leaving spreading ripples. *Sometimes, son,*

the shadows play their tricks. My dad had taught
a vanished floater might be a mirage,
and when squinting failed, you had to gauge
your line, the tension. If it wasn't taut

then there was dreaming. Say, of the time it took
to teach the proper way to set a hook.
Say, of an old canoe that used to sit
on a shore but found some way to drift.

Acknowledgments

My sincere gratitude to the editors of the journals in which the following poems first appeared, sometimes in a slightly different form:

Autumn Sky Poetry Daily: "Ice-out" *and* "With the Current"

Canary—A Literary Journal of the Environmental Crisis: "Exit 37B"

I-70 Review: "The Squannacook at Dawn"

Kestrel, A Journal of Literature and Art: "Upon Reading the Local Pages"

New York Quarterly: "Night Fishing with Otters"

The Road Not Taken: The Journal of Formal Poetry: "The Art of Topwater Fishing"

Rust & Moth: "First Caddis"

Sugar House Review: "Casting from Shore " and "Mackerel Day"

The Take 5ive Journal: [I lift the trout fly…]

Tar River Poetry: "Returning to Vermont" and "Spillage"

Third Wednesday Magazine: "Blackbird Through October Mist" and "Old Men Fishing, With Osprey"

Two Review: "Happy Meals"

Unbroken Journal—Prose Poems: "Jesus on the River"

Valparaiso Poetry Review: "Casting from Shore (II)" (published under the title "Casting")

Early Praise

Each of the twenty poems that comprise *The Squannacook at Dawn* is so well crafted that the art is all readers experience, the craft a scaffolding that has been removed. Each poem begins with a sense of welcome and closes unpredictably, yet inevitably (i.e., no better ending seems possible). This is high praise, but it's not my only reason for selecting this manuscript as winner of The Poetry Box Chapbook Prize for 2023. Read together and in the order they appear in the collection, these twenty poems create what feels like a twenty-first poem: the chapbook itself. The poet has not only written twenty fine poems—none an imitation of another in content or form—but when read straight through, the poems provide readers with a tightly woven and beautiful verbal tapestry, each poem contributing indelibly to the chapbook's larger context or story.

—Andrea Hollander, contest judge
and author of *And Now, Nowhere but Here*

The art of poetry and the art of fishing come together in these deeply felt, beautifully observed poems. The attentiveness to word and cadence speaks to and for all that the poet notices, be it river currents or dragonflies or ospreys. The earth and the waters are also very much speaking, and Richard Jordan has listened carefully. The scenarios vary as they reflect the amplitude of memorable occasions, but the aim is true in poem after poem—a sense of gratitude to be in the undiminished splendor that is out-of-doors.

—Baron Wormser, author of *The History Hotel*
and former Poet Laureate of Maine

The Squannacook at Dawn is the perfect antidote to an age of human beings anxiously awaiting the next ping of their cell phones. If you've ever wondered where fly fishers get their patience and why they don't get bored, the answer is clear in this vivid, wise collection. It's in poet Richard Jordan's dad, *an iridescent scale glued to his thumb/ glinting in the April morning sun*. These poems, some of them gently formal, others prose poems, dissolve the work week in the natural world's healing magic: egrets, otters, and of course, rainbow trout. Even Jesus prefers the river to the church here—not just for baptism but for beauty and peace. Jordan is at his best observing the specific: loosestrife, cognac pipe tobacco, Macoun apples, the "jug-o-rum" croak of a bullfrog, mist. Even if your dad never taught you how to tie a fly, you need to spend some time in the shade near the water with a copy of *The Squannacook at Dawn*.

—Christine Potter, author of *Unforgetting*
and *Sheltering in Place*

In *The Squannacook at Dawn*, Richard Jordan uses close observation of nature, strong memories, and exquisite language to evoke the holiness of fishing. He pulls the reader in with precise details such as in the poem, "Night Fishing with Otters," where he describes five young otters *at the edge of sedge and bulrush* and the mother otter with *a hefty, flapping catfish plucked/ from the mud*. Whether he's delineating moments spent fishing with his father, witnessing old men talking, or remembering a house that once stood by a creek, he leads the reader to feel at home in nature, to appreciate the fleeting beauty of the world.

—Judy Kaber, author of *Renaming the Seasons*
and former Poet Laureate of Belfast, Maine

About the Author

A Ph.D. mathematician by training and data scientist by vocation, Richard Jordan has been an avid reader of poetry for almost as long as he can remember and has been writing poetry for twenty years. His poems have appeared in many literary journals, including *Tar River Poetry, Rattle* (finalist for the 2022 *Rattle* Poetry Prize), *Little Patuxent Review, Sugar House Review, New York Quarterly, Autumn Sky Poetry Daily, Rappahannock Review* and *Valparaiso Poetry Review*. When not doing math or reading & writing poetry, he is most likely at a river or lake somewhere casting away. He resides in Littleton, Massachusetts, a short drive from the Squannacook River.

About The Poetry Box® Chapbook Prize

The Poetry Box® Chapbook Prize is open to both established poets and emerging talent alike. The contest is open to poets residing in the United States and is open for submissions each year during the month of February. Find more information at ThePoetryBox.com.

2023 Winners
The Squannacook at Dawn by Richard Jordan
Inside Out by Kirsten Morgan
Reading Wind by Carol Barrett

2022 Winners
Tracking the Fox by Rosalie Sanara Petrouske
Elemental Things by Michael S. Glaser
Listening in the Dark by Suzy Harris

2021 Winners
Erasures of My Coming Out (Letter) by Mary Warren Foulk
Of the Forest by Linda Ferguson
Let's Hear It for the Horses by Tricia Knoll

2020 Winners
The Day of My First Driving Lesson by Tiel Aisha Ansari
My Mother Never Died Before by Marcia B. Loughran
Off Coldwater Canyon by C.W. Emerson

2019 Winners
Moroccan Holiday by Lauren Tivey
Hello, Darling by Christine Higgins
Falling into the River by Debbie Hall

2018 Winners
Shrinking Bones by Judy K. Mosher
November Quilt by Penelope Scambly Schott
14: Antología del Sonoran by Christopher Bogart
Fireweed by Gudrun Bortman

www.ingramcontent.com/pod-product-compliance
Lightning Source LLC
LaVergne TN
LVHW051057100526
838202LV00087BA/6987